10 Creativity Lessons through Short Stories

Contents

Curiosity is Key

this story encourages you to ask questions and be creative. It teaches you the value of curiosity and how it can help you learn new things and solve problems.

the Curious Kitten

In a small town, there was a curious kitten named Milo. Milo loved to explore and learn new things. One day, he was walking down the street when he saw a group of birds flying high in the sky. "Wow! How do they fly?" Milo wondered. He wanted to know more about it, so he decided to ask his friend, a wise old owl.

"Hello, Mr. Owl," said Milo. "Can you tell me how birds fly?"

the wise old owl smiled and said, "Of course, Milo. Birds have light but strong bones that help them fly. They also have powerful muscles that allow them to move their wings quickly." Milo was amazed by this information. He thanked the wise old owl and went on his way, eager to learn more.

Over time, Milo became known as the most curious kitten in town. He asked questions about everything he saw, heard, and felt. He learned so much that he started solving problems that no one else could. One day, he discovered a solution to a big problem in his town.

His curious mind had helped him find the answer. From that day on, everyone in town respected Milo for his curiosity and problem-solving skills.

Message: By being curious and asking questions, you can learn new things and solve problems. This skill will benefit you in the future when you face challenges that require creative and innovative solutions.

Find Beauty in Everyday things

this story teaches you to observe the world around you and appreciate the beauty in things. It encourages you to develop a sense of curiosity and wonder about the world around you.

the Magic of Nature

In a small, peaceful village lived a curious young girl named Luna. She loved exploring the world around her and observing all the things in nature. One day, while walking through the forest, she noticed a beautiful butterfly fluttering by. Luna was in awe of the butterfly's vibrant colors and delicate wings. She followed the butterfly as it flitted from flower to flower, observing its graceful flight and admiring the way it moved.

As she watched the butterfly, she noticed other things too: the soft rustling of wind through the leaves, the chirping of the birds, and the glistening of dew drops on the petals of a flower. Luna marveled at the beauty of all the minute details she had never noticed before.

After watching the butterfly for a while, Luna continued on her path, looking at the world around her with newfound appreciation. She noticed the way the trees swayed in the wind, the sparkle of sunlight on a stream, and the intricate patterns on a butterfly's wing.

Luna realized that there was so much more to the world than she had ever known before. By simply paying attention and observing the trivial things around her, she discovered a whole new world of beauty.

Message: By observing the world around you and appreciating the beauty in things, you can develop a sense of wonder and curiosity. This skill will benefit you in the future as you learn new things and explore the world around you.

Boldly Experiment

This story encourages you to experiment and take risks in your learning and problem-solving. It teaches you the value of trying new things and taking chances, even if you are unsure of the outcome.

the Little Scientist

In a small village by the hills, there lives a curious and adventurous girl named Ava. Ava had always been interested in science, and she spent most of her time experimenting and discovering new things.

One day, while walking in the village, Ava saw a problem in the community. the nearby river was polluted, and it was affecting the fish population and the vegetation around it. Ava knew that the situation needed a solution, but she did not have one yet.

Being a little scientist, Ava decided to experiment and try new things. She mixed different chemicals, tried different cleaning methods, and even tested the water's quality herself. She tried and failed many times, but she never gave up.

Finally, after many attempts and failures, Ava discovered a solution that worked. She found a bio-remediation technique that helped clean the river without harming the fish or plants. She was proud of her accomplishment and happily shared her solution with the village community.

From that day on, Ava became known as the little scientist in the village. She was respected and admired for her passion and her bravery in trying new things and taking risks.

Message: By experimenting and taking risks in your learning and problem-solving, you can discover new things and find innovative solutions to problems. this skill will benefit you in the future as you face challenges and problems that require creative and innovative solutions.

Express Yourself

this story teaches you to express yourself in different ways, including drawing, writing, painting, singing, and dancing. It encourages you to explore your creativity and discover new ways to express yourself.

the Artist's Canvas

In a small town, there lived a young boy named Max who loved to draw. He spent most of his time with his sketchbook, drawing pictures of everything around him. He loved the way drawing allowed him to express himself in a unique and personal way.

One day, Max met a group of kids who shared his passion for art. They loved to paint, sing, and dance, and they invited Max to join them in their artistic pursuits. Max was hesitant at first, as he had never drawn before, but he decided to try it.

Max discovered that he loved painting, singing, and dancing as much as he loved drawing. Each form of expression brought a new dimension to his creativity, allowing him to see the world in different ways.

He painted pictures of the sky and the sea, sang songs about love and friendship, and danced to the rhythm of the music. He felt free and alive, expressing himself in ways he had never thought possible.
Max and his friends continued to explore their creativity, expressing themselves in new and exciting ways. They drew, painted, sang, and danced to their hearts' content, delighting in the colorful and vibrant world they had created.

Message: By expressing yourself in different ways, you can explore your creativity and discover new ways to communicate and express your ideas and emotions. This skill will benefit you in the future as you learn to effectively express yourself in various situations.

Collaborate and Communicate

this story teaches you the importance of collaboration and listening to others' ideas. It encourages you to work together and respect each other's opinions when solving problems.

the Puzzle With Friends

One sunny day, a group of friends got together to solve a giant puzzle. They were excited to get started and wanted to finish it quickly. The friends worked hard but soon realized that the puzzle was much harder than they thought. They were stuck on a particular part of the puzzle and could not find the missing pieces. They felt frustrated and unhappy. One of the friends, named Lily, had an idea.

She suggested that they listen to each other's ideas and work together to solve the puzzle. Everyone agreed, and they began to share their ideas.

One suggested that they check under the table, and another said to look on the ground. Lily had something else in mind. She suggested that they each go back and look at different parts of the puzzle they had worked on.

As they went back to their respective areas, they discovered that they had missed a few pieces under the table and in a corner. When they put the pieces together, the puzzle was finally complete! the friends were ecstatic that they had solved the puzzle by working together and listening to each other's ideas.

Message: Collaboration and listening to others' ideas are important skills that you will need as you grow up. When you work together and respect each other's opinions, you can solve problems and achieve your goals more effectively and efficiently.

Challenge Assumptions

this story encourages you to challenge assumptions and think critically about different opinions and ideas. It teaches you the importance of questioning assumptions and considering multiple perspectives.

the Mystery of the Missing toy

One afternoon, a group of kids were playing with their toys in the park. A little boy named Jack brought his favorite toy car but soon realized that it was missing. He looked everywhere but could not find it.

the other kids began to share their opinions about where the toy car could be. Some thought it had been stolen, while others thought it was just misplaced. But Jack was not satisfied with the guesses of his friends. He wanted to find his car and needed a proper solution.

So Jack decided to think critically about the situation and challenge assumptions. He asked questions like:
"Is there any evidence that the car was stolen?"
"Could it be under the grass or lost inside the garden?"
"Did I bring my car to the park, or did I leave it at home?"

By asking these questions and considering different perspectives, Jack discovered that the toy car had been left at home and that he had forgotten to bring it to the park.

the kids were amazed by Jack's critical thinking abilities and thanked him for teaching them to challenge assumptions and consider different perspectives.

Message: By challenging assumptions and thinking critically about different opinions and ideas, you can find solutions to problems and make better decisions. this skill will benefit you in the future as you face challenges that require analytical and logical thinking.

Storytelling Sparks Imagination

this story helps you develop your storytelling skills as it promotes imagination and creativity. It encourages you to use your imagination and creativity to develop stories and share them with others.

the Magic Pen

there was a young girl named Maya who loved to draw. She was so good at it that her drawings often looked like they were coming to life. One day, while working on a drawing, Maya noticed something strange. A tiny, glittering pen had appeared on her desk.

As she picked up the pen, she realized that it was no ordinary pen. It was a magic pen that could bring her drawings to life. She began to draw a beautiful forest with streams, birds, and animals, and as she drew, the landscape began to come alive.

As the forest came to life, Maya found herself transported to a magical world filled with adventures and mysteries. She took her magic pen everywhere and drew amazing stories that she could share with others.

Maya discovered that she could create and tell stories through her drawings and writing. She realized that everyone has a story to tell and that by expressing herself creatively, she could share her stories with the world.

Message: By developing your storytelling skills, you can promote your imagination and creativity. You can create an amazing world full of magic and adventure that you can share with your friends and family. this skill would benefit you in the future by improving your communication and writing abilities, which will help you convey your thoughts and ideas more effectively.

Learning is Limitless

this story encourages you to learn multiple subjects, not just your favorites. It teaches you the importance of exploring and learning various subjects, as they can help you with your future career and personal growth.

the Adventure of a Lifetime

There once was a young boy named Luke who loved sports. He spent most of his time playing football, basketball, and hockey. Luke loved these sports and was incredibly good at them, but he did not enjoy school and thought that it was a waste of time.

One day, a new teacher came to their school and introduced them to different subjects like science, history, and geography. At first, Luke was not interested, but the teacher made the classes fun and engaging, and soon Luke began to enjoy learning more.

As he began to explore new subjects, Luke discovered that he had a passion for science and even history. He started to read more books, watch videos about science, and learn about how much science and math are used in sports.

By learning different subjects, Luke began to see a whole new world of possibilities. He realized that many careers combined his love of sports with his new interest in science and history, and he felt excited about his potential future. Luke started to work harder and study more. He discovered that mastering different subjects helps to improve his critical thinking, problem-solving, and communication skills, which are essential not only for his future studies and career but also in daily life.

Message: Learning multiple subjects such as science, history, and geography helps you expand your horizons and improve your academic performance. It encourages you to explore your interests and passions, and it can open new opportunities and career paths in the future.

Embrace Failure

this story teaches you to push through failures and see them as opportunities for growth. It encourages you to never give up on your dreams and to embrace challenges as opportunities for personal growth.

the Little Seed's Journey

Once, in a field of flowers, there was a small seed that dreamed of growing into a beautiful flower. However, when it tried to grow, it faced many challenges. The soil was too dry, the sun was too hot, and it was often trampled on by the animals.

Despite all these hardships, the little seed never gave up on its dream of becoming a flower. It pushed through the failures, using every experience as an opportunity to grow.

The little seed continued to grow with perseverance, and it was not long before it became a strong sapling that grew into a beautiful and colorful flower. The other flowers in the field were amazed by the little seed's journey and how it never gave up on its dream, even when it faced numerous challenges.

The little seed taught them that failure is not an obstacle but a stepping stone to success. Every challenge provides an opportunity for growth, and every step toward our dreams counts, no matter how small.

Message: Every challenge we face in life is an opportunity for growth and personal development. You should learn to push through failures and see them as steps toward your goals. It helps build resilience, problem-solving, and decision-making skills that are important for facing future obstacles. With perseverance and a positive attitude, you can achieve anything you set your mind to.

Seek New Experiences

this story inspires you to seek out new experiences and form new connections with people, places, and things to spark your creativity. It encourages you to explore the world around you and become more adventurous.

Explore to Learn

Alex was a young boy who loved adventure and creativity. He was always looking for new experiences and was never afraid to try something new.

One day, Alex decided to explore the world around him. He started by taking a walk around his neighborhood, and he discovered new things that he had never seen before. He met new people, saw new places, and learned new things.

Alex's curiosity and adventurous spirit took him on many amazing adventures. He explored local parks, tried new foods, read books about far-off lands, and learned about different cultures.

Through all these experiences, Alex discovered that new connections spark his creativity. He started to paint, draw, and write amazing stories about his adventures. His creativity and imagination soared, and he felt more alive than ever before.

Alex realized that creativity is not just about what you do but also how you do it. New experiences help to broaden our horizons, and exploring new places and things can open whole new worlds of possibilities.

Message: Seeking out new experiences and forming new connections helps spark creativity and allows us to explore the world around us. You should be encouraged to step outside your comfort zone to grow and be more adventurous in your daily lives. This skill will benefit you in the future as you continue to explore and learn in new ways, creating new and exciting possibilities.

Made in United States
Troutdale, OR
07/21/2024

21240254R00017